D1799299

TIDES AND STONE WALLS

BY THE SAME AUTHOR

Fiction
Saturday Night and Sunday Morning
The Loneliness of the Long Distance Runner
The General
Key to the Door
The Ragman's Daughter
The Death of William Posters
A Tree on Fire
Guzman, Go Home
A Start in Life
Travels in Nihilon
Raw Material
Men, Women and Children
The Flame of Life
The Widower's Son
The Storyteller
The Second Chance and Other Stories
Her Victory
The Lost Flying Boat
Down From the Hill
Life Goes On

Poetry
The Rats and Other Poems
A Falling Out of Love and Other Poems
Love in the Environs of Voronezh
Storm and Other Poems
Snow on the North Side of Lucifer
Sun Before Departure

Plays
All Citizens are Soldiers (with Ruth Fainlight)
Three Plays

Essays
Mountains and Caverns

For Children
The City Adventures of Marmalade Jim
Big John and the Stars
The Incredible Fencing Fleas
Marmalade Jim on the Farm
Marmalade Jim and the Fox

TIDES AND STONE WALLS

Poems by

ALAN SILLITOE

Photographs by Victor Bowley

GRAFTON BOOKS
A Division of the Collins Publishing Group

LONDON GLASGOW
TORONTO SYDNEY AUCKLAND

Grafton Books
A Division of the Collins Publishing Group
8 Grafton Street, London W1X 3LA

Published by Grafton Books 1986

Text copyright © 1986 by Alan Sillitoe
Photographs copyright © 1986 by Victor Bowley

British Library Cataloguing in Publication Data

Sillitoe, Alan
 Tides and stone walls.
 I.Title
 821'.914   PR6037.I55

ISBN 0 246 12717 1

Printed in Great Britain by
Mackays of Chatham Limited

All rights reserved. No part of this publication may be
reproduced, stored in a retrieval system, or transmitted,
in any form or by any means, electronic, mechanical,
photocopying, recording or otherwise, without the prior
permission of the publisher.

In memory of
my sister Pearl

Contents

TIDES AND STONE WALLS

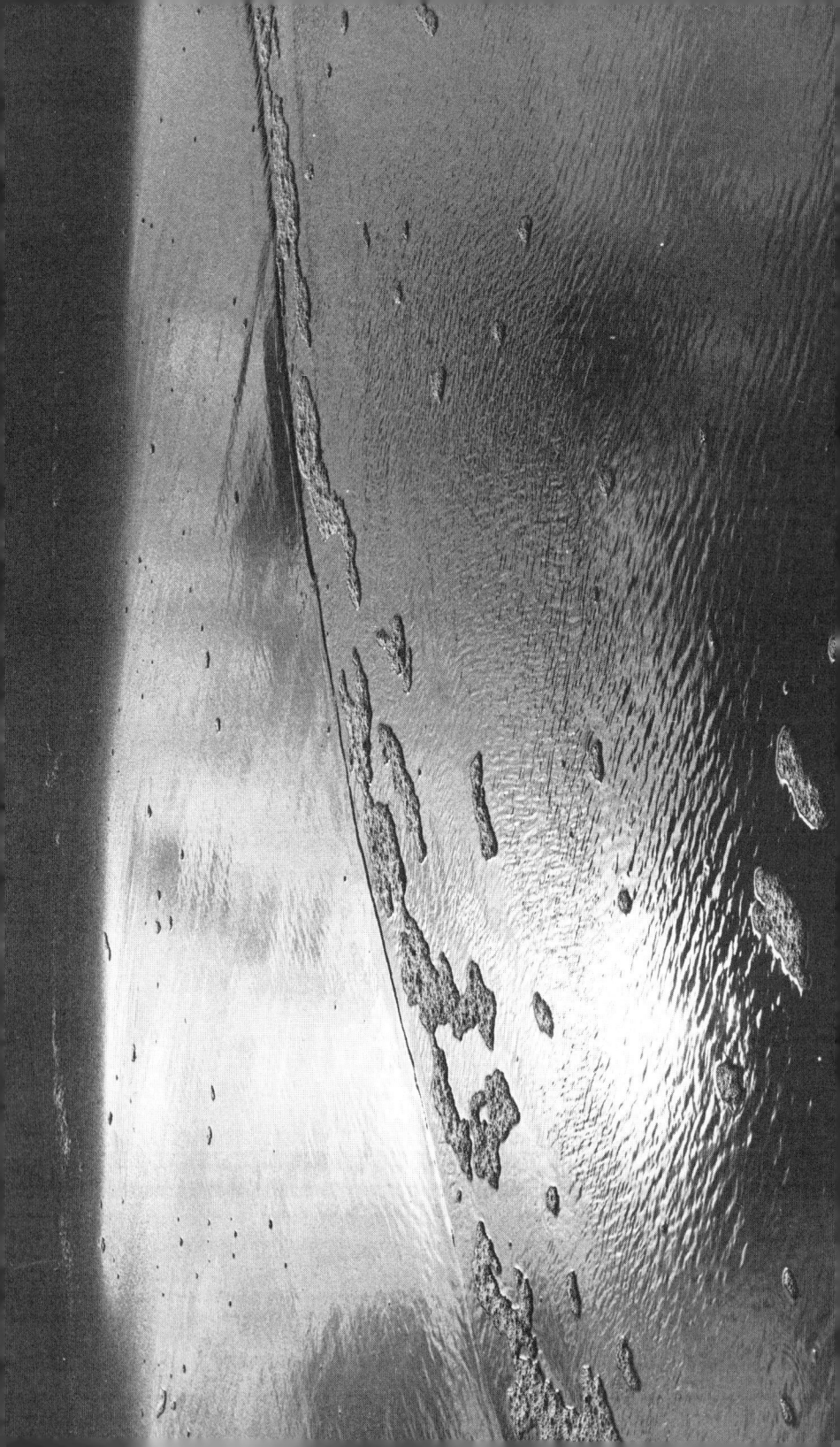

Receding Tide

The tide is fickle.
After going out it comes back.
The moon sees to that.

It's what the tide reveals
When it huffs and leaves
That means so much;

And what the tide covers
On nibbling back
That opens our eyes.

Archipelagoes left unexplored
And rivers unsurveyed
Are given to our view:

But before the meaning's known
The regimental rush of waves
Is preceded by
The brutal skirmishing of dreams.

Bricks

Bricks build walls
They erect houses
Both rise up
Men make them out of earth and clay.
Water tightens them
Ovens bake them to withstand
Bullets and dour weather.

Rectilinear and hard
Red or blue
Porous or solid
Beautifully stacked:
They invite the mason's hand
To choose.
The natural enemy of bricks
Are bombs.

Stroke them tenderly,
And share their warmth.

Esplanade Hotel at Seaford

The Esplanade Hotel
With fifty rooms in 1927
From six-and-six a night
Shone like fifty lighthouses.

It was passion's workhouse
For Mr and Mrs Smith
From Brighton's overspill,
And worked wonders

For self-made captains
And their ladies
Doing the resorts
By boat or motor.

Money was money
When you had it,
And prices cheap.
The Esplanade Hotel was cosy,

Each wall a thousand
Built-in groans.
Ceilings were jewelled with laughter
But problems padded the floors.

Farces crumbled to dust
When they pulled it down.
Anguish scooped by the ton
Was taken away in dumper trucks.

Happiness was food
In the gullet of a seagull
That spun between
The sun and water.

Metal Object on Beach

Stones within the circumvallation
Want to get out.
Others strive to enter.
Life is a prison.

Those craving to escape
Fight with clamourers breaking in.
Prison is life.

Who first laid out the palisade?
Stones wait patiently
For a wind to blow it away.

If and when,
It will land somewhere else.
Life goes on.

Landscape – Sennon, Cornwall

How many died when this height was taken?
Upslope the armoured horses went:
Old refurbished iron-men
Zig-zagging from rocks
And knights already fallen.

The cunning defenders
Jabbed soft underbellies,
Brought riders down
On gleaming daggers.

Victors mourned
As the defeated King rode
Into rain beyond the hill.

Blood makes history,
And desolation
A winter's day.

Low Tide   Leigh on Sea

All that is left of a winter's day
Is a strip of water and a mile of mud.
Sea has stranded the exhausted fleet.

A wooden gangway crosses sand,
Patches made by seaboots going home.
What semaphoric signals called them in?

Boarded Window   Hastings

If I rip those planks back
Will I see
Something new, or out of nature?

Years ago I put them on,
Felt glee in my fist
As I swung the hammer
And saw each nail
Biting into seasoned wood.

I didn't know then what I boarded up
Sunlight on the beach
Pebbles in my palms
Grass in my teeth
An upturned rowing boat;

Thumb and forefinger held the nail.
I laughed at something new
Or out of nature.
They paid me – though not too well.

If I have the strength (or tools)
To lever off those planks
My soul will dazzle me with grief,
And out of my own nature blind me
With what I boarded up.

Window — Sennon Cove

A window sets the battle lines
Between geometry and fantasy –
Would hem in the world if it were square
And the mind without limits.

A window squarely poses
Whether to look in
Or go through:
Outside is entertainment;
Within, there's trouble.

Whether to observe or live
Is the question.
You can't do both.
When a window stares at you
Till you become a window
Your gift flies backwards through it,
And leaves no option but to live.

Stay clear of windows.

Broken Windows, Southend

Eyes down: look in.
Eyes up: see a window.
Break it to hear
The shattering glass concerto
By Bullet Bomb or Fist –
The three great soloists.

Applaud: dust will do the rest.
A cat will have its kittens.
A man on the tramp will open the door
To drink his purloined parsnip beer
Then throw his empty bottle at the wall,
And dream his nightmare dream against the wind
Of kittens sleeping on his face.
He'll wake
And in anguish smash
Windows which won't look at him,
Down to the final square of unspecked glass.

A long walk lies ahead.

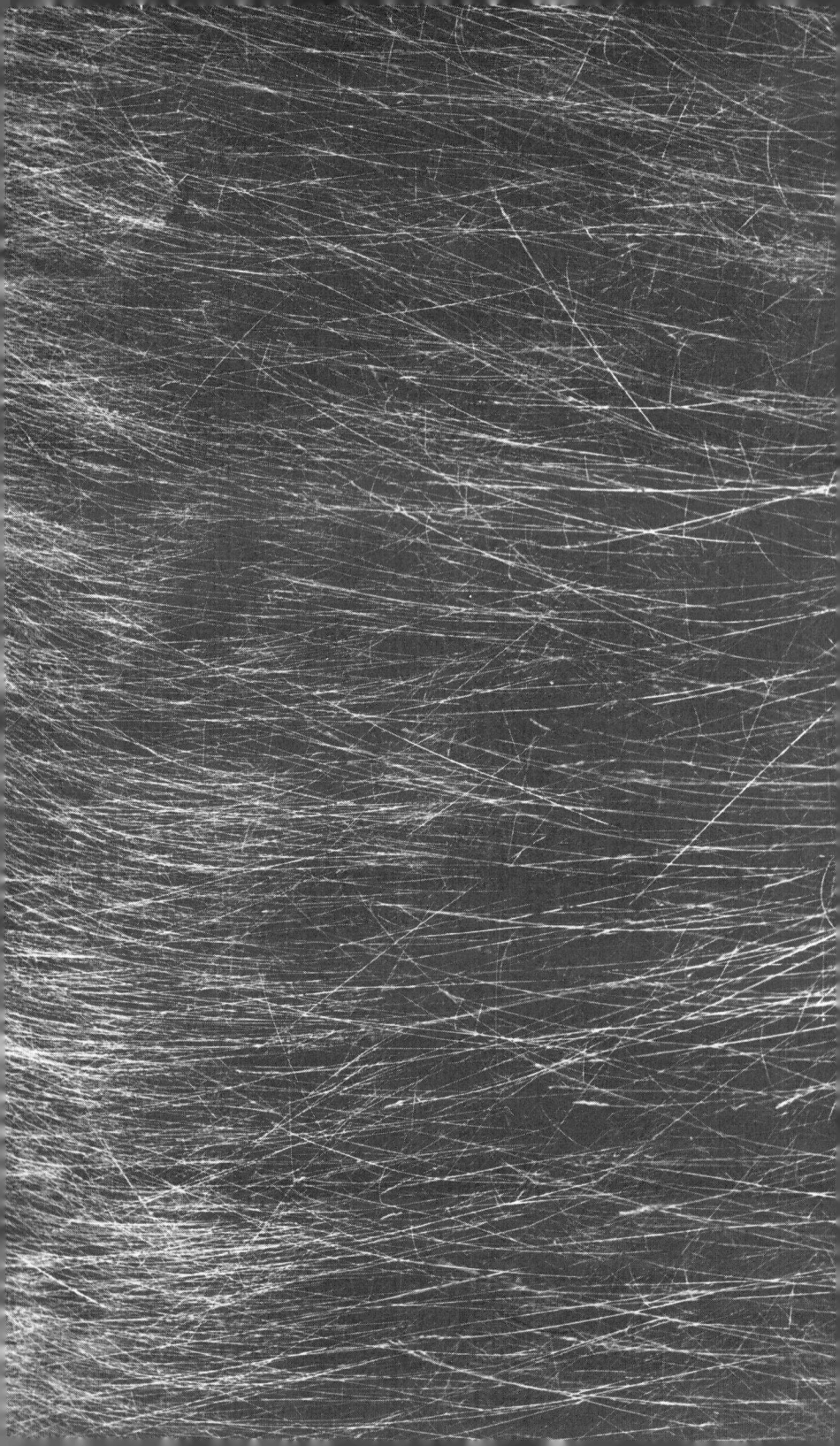

Long Grass — Seaford Head

Be considerate to coastal grass.
It's not as gentle as you think.
Pull it roughly
And your palm is scraped.
A bundle will scour pots clean.

Thatch a hut
Or make a hat,
But look at your feet
On walking through
In case a snake uncoils;

Or lie in it and be concealed,
Make your sweetheart happy
On her bed of Eden-grass.

Window of Fisherman's Shed, Hastings

Door
Or gate?
Don't tell me it's a window.
Depends who looks, and why.

I've seen it before:
Land or sea-creature
Laughs from the moon.

The face that sees them
Had its features burnt
Turned into this square door
Gate
Window,

A soul tormented in the moonlight
Forever.

The Ground near Lifeboat House, Hastings

Follow me.
I don't ask where you come from:
Someone who already walked this way
Stamped a broken battleaxe
For every following foot to follow.
Don't ask where to.

Walk on:
As long as you can hear the sea
To one side or the other.
The pattern-maker's smile says:
The same end waits for everyone.

Palace Pier, Brighton, Winter 1982

I met her on this pier.
Which plank her foot stood on
What pillar she leaned against
I only know she looked inland
Over her shoulder I saw the sea.

We promised to live forever
I saw a ship between two kisses
Going up and down for France.
She opened her eyes and saw a bus
We didn't care who saw us.

For thirty years we laughed or wept
Scorched, sea-wracked, wind-blown
We kept it going
And now come back to see
Paint peeled off and planks gone rotten.

Underneath, the sea still boils.

Drain Cover, Pinner

We often wondered where he'd gone.
He left one Friday after dinner.
I'm going to buy some fags.
He *had* been getting thinner.

Well, not all that thin,
We said when it was too late.
It was raining as well, and foggy.
He just slipped down a fever grate.

There's no moral in it.
I suppose he went to sea,
Working tankers off the China Coast.
Will he never come back to tea?

Maybe one day he'll climb out of that grate
(When the sewers are in full spate)
And, not much thinner,
Knock on the door and wink for his dinner!

Derelict Bathing Cabins at Seaford

Well, they would, wouldn't they?
They'd say anything.
Doris and Betty got undressed.
Bob and Fred did the same next door.
The things that went on in these changing huts.
Well, with the war over what could you expect?
They came back like new men.
Well, they came back.
They came, anyway.
Sometimes it was you and my Fred.
Sometimes it was me and your Bob.
It was nice with us, though, wasn't it?
Nothing but a clean bit of fun.
Sad they both went in a year of each other –
The dirty devils!
Nothing but a clean bit of fun,
When we changed into our costumes,
The sea washed it off, though, didn't it?
We had some good swims as well.
And now look how they've smashed 'em up.
Poor old bathing huts.
Never be the same again.
The sea chucked all them pebbles in.
Don't suppose it liked the goings on.
Then the vandals ripped the doors off.
They didn't like it, either.
The old times never come back,
But at least we 'ad 'em!

Pebbles on the Beach at Cuckmere Haven

Sun quiet. Sea quiet.
Geological alert.
How could that be?

Radio taps the tidings out
Of how two quiet regions
Could be put on GEO ALERT.

Stones don't care
On a beach of shingle-dingle
When you walk.

Nor you and me. They go up
And they come down.
So do we.

Stones forever at our feet
Lay in their perfect places
When we have gone.

Fisherman's Hut, Hastings

A fisherman's hut is
Neptune's office,
A fishy filing system
In tumbled boxes on a shelf;
The riot act
Unread forever;
The be-all and end-all
Of bye-laws
Framed on the wall
Away from rats.

Wood pickled by sea salt
And the smoke of pipes.
In Neptune's office
The brandy in its
Bottle is tucked away
In a woollen jumper
For instant readiness.

Sea and Sky at Land's End

Marconi waited for his morse
Mystically
To bark its route from Newfoundland.
It did. The sky was good to him,
And to ships' crews in travail
Beyond Land's End.

The cumulo-nimbus view enthralls
But atmospherics mangle
Dots-and-dashes
Crying to save our ship.

The sun is a box of golden powder
Shaken on the sea,
And scattered by thunder
Into good night.

Cockleshells

The world is overpopulated
Even by cockleshells
On the seashore.

If there was one left
It would buy brides and cattle
Or be in a museum.

Victims of proliferation are food
Their remnants crunched
When boots tread by.

Aeons turn a slipshod slug
Into a cockle, a homely name
For the harmless *cardium edule*.

Walls

Walls made with stones of the field
Are more permanent and closer to the earth
Than those brick-built;
Harder to see
On a hillside of your compass-bearing.
Loose stones damage careless hikers
Who must find a gate, a gap,
Or stepping-place to get over.

Walls give employment to scattered stones
Which stop crops growing;
Guard succulent grass
From flattening by gales,
Hold sheep from roaming,
Are made for leaning on
Or talking to your neighbour.
They divide and fortify,
Can be a nuisance –
But have their uses.

Hole in Fence, Greenwich

Holes were never much bigger,
But big enough:
The jagged rip
An early wink of light leavening the darkness
Of Day One at school.

The Biblical needle
The lockless keyhole
The steady eye
Or broken door,

Kept in mind year after year
A secret put away
But sometimes taken out and looked at
Like a prize gained in a past life,
Then slid back with a smile
Till despair hauled it out again.

No question as to how it got there:
The hole did not increase in size like you.
Your years stood behind until
So many and strong,
They one day pushed you through,
And you were free.

Mousehole, Cornwall. Garage Door

Who lives at Number Twelve?
Mr John Dough-Dekker
With the trembling knees:
He'd once been tough and rich –
Born on an island
In the Dodecanese.

The flimsy bolt of Number Twelve
Was rattled by kids en route for school,
And old John unmistakably saw
Through one of the spyholes in that thin door
Martin Rattler and Mischievous Kate
Kick at his garage like any old gate –
And like elvers snake away.

He shook a fist at his boxwood door
Then donned a sporty travelling cap
Climbed up into his motorcar,
And with trembling knees let go the brake,
He ran a finger over the towns
On his tattered touring map;
But he never drove out of the garage,
For he'd been everywhere before.

Kensal Green Cemetery

You plant dead people
And monuments come up.

Were folk so bad
In their lives
That soil
Works harder
Than they once did,
Producing stone
Instead of flesh?

With no light to see by
They give stone monuments
As fully formed as babies.

Southend Pier, November

A pier is a bridge that failed
You might say,
Whatever else is said.

At the end are fish, and ships
And underneath is water,
Or jewelled shingle.

Lamp posts point to the signal station
So does the toytown railway.
People buy and sell.

The planks smell fresh.
Not liking salt
They reach for land.

A rotund father and thin daughter
Stroll by hand-in-hand.
Good for business.

A walking-stick clatters
But don't look now:
The invisible man goes by.

Every pier has one.
He swaggers to the end and back,
Panama hat at an angle;

And then again returns,
Craving land beyond the water,
Condemned to walk forever.

Tin Surface, Fence

The sergeant-major-domo lit
The match.
The circus crowd was as quiet
As the tentflaps.

Only the moustache flipped
Away from the flame.
The hoop was set afire
And waited, like us all.

The angle of elevation set
Should have shot him through
And into the safety net.
But a sudden throaty roar

From the lions' pen next door
Twitched the muzzle and upset
The range and angle
"And every damned thing" –

The sergeant-major-domo sobbed in court.
Once ejected
The human cannonball
Described a fairly graceful curvature

Almost too quick to see,
Shot through the tent
And rent the air.
From the attic of a boarding house

A man in shirtsleeves saw him plough
And zoom right through the fence,
Which left the jagged tin-rip
Gaping forever at such passersby
As you. And me.

Plaster Wall

Man's ingenuity to man
Is immeasurable, and sure.
He does it for himself
But shares with others,
Often for money, because he has to,
And out of pride perhaps.

Kings make Pyramids
Or Persian fortresses
Or the Taj Mahal
Or the wall around Jerusalem;

But artisans thatch roofs
Plaster walls with skill
And set up airtight buildings
For chiefs to plan fantastic schemes in –

Of Pyramids and Persian fortresses
And the wall around Jerusalem,
Visible forever.
But humbler walls crumble,
And only for a moment
Leave us with their traces.

Houses at Whitechapel

We came off the ship:
"This is America. You're here!"
A shorter crossing
Than the railway trip.
Having a living to make,
It was better than Russia
Because nobody tried to kill us.

America was smaller than we thought.
We lived three generations
In that house:
New Year
Atonement
Passover.

Bricks talk,
But Books are eloquent.

After Rough Sea, at Seaford

He went to sea because he didn't like the dark.
He wanted his ship to be looked at from the shore
By a woman who would wonder
Where he was going and why
But not where coming from:
His mother;

And stared at by a man who envied him
And craved to follow:
His father.

Many do not like the dark
But on a ship at night the light stays on
Inside yourself.
You take it like a mother into you
In case the sun won't show at dawn.

At sea there's only
Space, and you.

Rock Pool, Isle of Barra

Our flying boat, scraping the Narrows,
Made a landing in the island's lee
And anchored in the bay;

Or you can say we overflew:
The Rock Pool felt our silhouette.
We took away the Rock Pool's picture.

Which alternative would leave
A firmer touch –
The Rock Pool disturbed
Or our uncertainty?

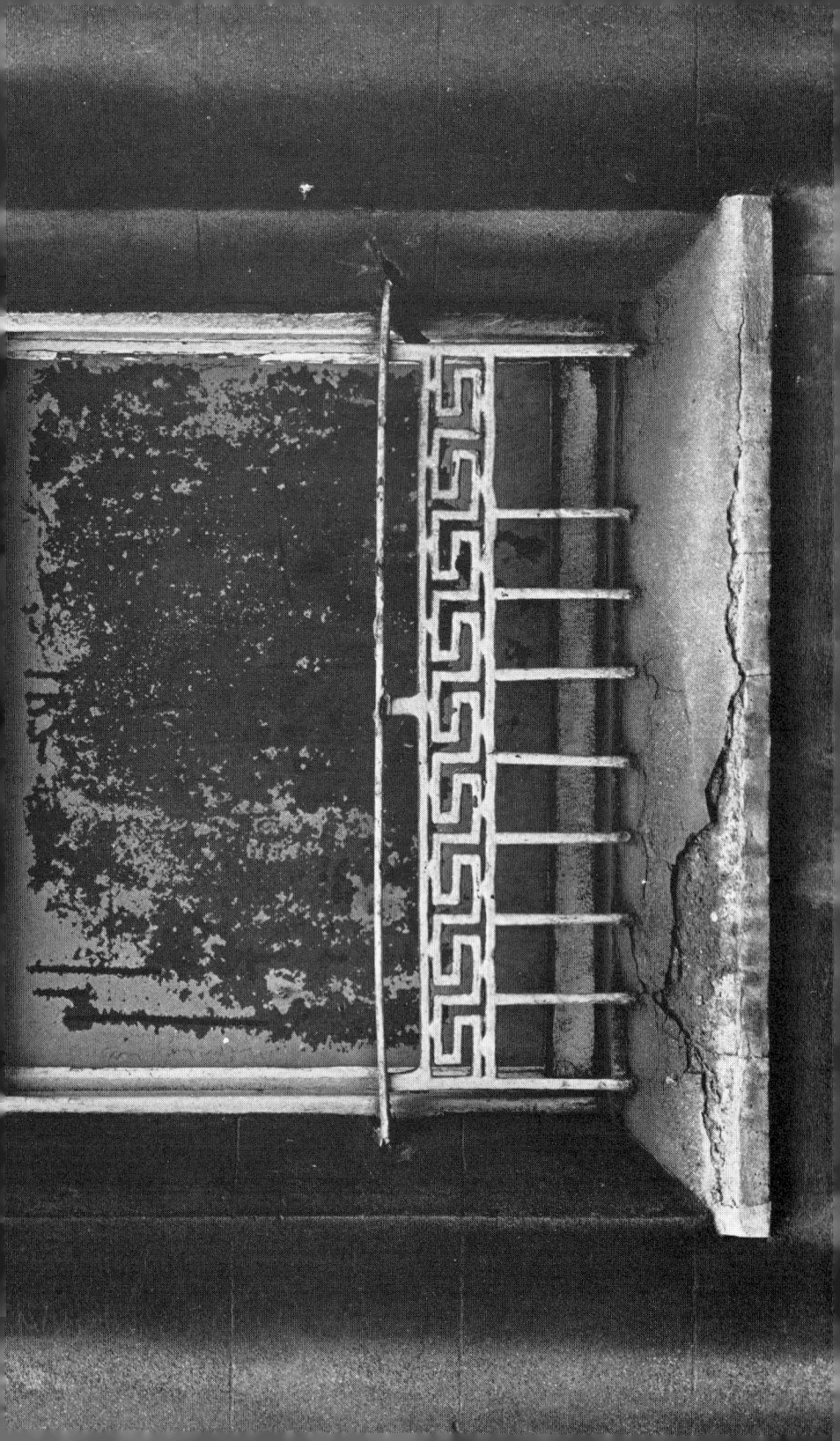

Window, Brighton

After thirty years he came home.
He'd forgotten the house
But recognised the window.

His sister never married
But she knew he'd come.
They passed unknowing in the Lanes.

The first iron dewdrop of the knocker
Shook dust
From the flowers.

Not today! she said.
He walked away,
Forgot the house

Forgot the window
Forgot his sister never married
Forgot the knocker made no sound

When it struck home.

Torn Poster — Venice

The Big Voice, the Visual Scream
Shouts about the National Lottery
Or the advantage of travelling by Aeroflot
Or the holiness of the Virgin's Grotto
Or a film about the antics
At the court of King Otto;
Or did someone win
A Motto competition –
First prize a reproduction
On a theme by Watteau?

Or, taking it all in all (and altogether)
Let's have a scenario like this:
The Big Bang Lottery Prize
Is a trip by Aeroflotto
To the Virgin's Grotto
In a corner of the crumbling Empire
Of crazy King Otto –
From which you come back, if at all
(You've guessed it) BLOTTO;
Crossing the frontier in a haycart
Concealed inside the wrappings
Of a cracker Motto
Against an idealised backdroppo
As designed by Watteau.

Speculation is a deadend
Painted in a Dresden Jar.
Forget it. A mindless hand
A single rip: we'll never know
Where poster-dreams
(And demons that lurk behind them) go.

Tiled Wall   Derelict Station, Uxbridge

Powdered Portland Stone
And Dorset sand
Conveniently mixed with water
Make a palimpsest of wet cement,
Inviting passersby
Surreptitiously to sport a
Go at patternising on its surface.

Who scratched the first design
On this tramp's Rosetta Stone
Cannot be said:
But scrawls that dried before another came
Find themselves by chance
Immortalised within a photo-frame.